Made in United States
North Haven, CT
16 October 2021

10364721R00057